# AI Property Analysis & Deal Evaluation

## How to Use AI to Analyze Cash Flow, ROI, and Risk in Seconds

*By Joe Correa*

Published by Live Stronger Faster



This book is for educational and informational purposes only. The author and publisher are not engaged in rendering legal, financial, or other professional advice. Readers should consult a qualified professional before making any financial decisions.

First Edition

# Table of Contents

# Introduction

This book marks a critical turning point in your journey through the AI Real Estate Investing Series because this is where investing stops being guesswork and becomes precision-based decision making. Up to this point, you have learned how artificial intelligence is reshaping the real estate landscape in general and how to identify opportunities using AI-driven lead generation systems. But now you step into the most important skill of all—understanding whether a deal is actually worth pursuing before you ever commit capital, time, or energy. This is the stage where most investors either accelerate their wealth building or lose money by relying on emotion, outdated assumptions, or incomplete analysis. AI changes that entirely by giving you the ability to evaluate properties with speed, accuracy, and a level of insight that was previously only available to institutional investors with large research teams.

At the core of this book is the understanding that every real estate deal is fundamentally a data problem. The property itself is not just a structure; it is a collection of numbers, inputs, and variables that determine whether it generates income, breaks even, or becomes a liability. These variables include purchase price, rental income potential, expenses, market conditions, appreciation trends, repair costs, vacancy rates, financing terms, and exit strategies. Traditionally, analyzing all of these factors required spreadsheets, manual research, and a high level of experience. Even then, results were often inconsistent because human analysis is limited by speed, bias, and incomplete data. AI removes those limitations by processing thousands of data points in seconds and presenting you with clear, structured insights that allow you to make decisions with confidence instead of uncertainty.

The first major transformation you will experience in this book is the shift from reactive analysis to real-time decision intelligence. Instead of analyzing deals after they come to you, you will learn how to instantly evaluate opportunities as they appear in your pipeline. AI deal calculators become your foundation, allowing you to input basic property information and immediately receive structured outputs such as cash flow projections, ROI estimates, break-even timelines, and risk assessments. These tools are not just calculators; they are intelligent systems that simulate real-world investment outcomes based on historical data, market trends, and predictive modeling. This means you are no longer relying on static assumptions—you are working with dynamic forecasts that adjust based on real market behavior.

Rental projections are one of the most powerful elements within this system because they determine the income side of your investment equation. In traditional investing, rental estimates are often based on comparable properties or general market averages, which can be misleading or outdated. AI, however, analyzes multiple data sources simultaneously, including rental listings, occupancy trends, seasonal fluctuations, neighborhood demand shifts, and historical rental performance. This allows you to understand not just what a property can rent for today, but how that rental income may evolve over time. This forward-looking perspective is what separates basic investors from strategic portfolio builders who understand long-term wealth creation.

Another critical area covered in this book is ARV estimation, or After Repair Value. This is especially important for investors involved in fix-and-flip strategies or value-add opportunities. Determining what a property will be worth after renovations has always been one of the most challenging aspects of real estate investing because it requires predicting market response to improvements. AI simplifies this process by analyzing comparable sales, renovation impact patterns, neighborhood appreciation rates, and buyer behavior data. Instead of relying on subjective guesses or limited comps, you gain a structured valuation model that gives you a much clearer picture of potential profit margins before you ever begin a project. Risk scoring is another essential component of AI-powered property analysis, and it represents one of the most powerful advancements in modern investing systems. Every real estate deal carries risk, whether it is related to financing, market volatility, tenant stability, property condition, or liquidity. Traditionally, investors had to mentally weigh these risks without a standardized system. AI introduces a consistent scoring model that evaluates multiple risk factors simultaneously and assigns a structured risk profile to each deal. This allows you to compare opportunities objectively rather than emotionally. Over time, this leads to better decision-making patterns, fewer costly mistakes, and a more stable investment portfolio.

The tools introduced in this book, DealCheck and Mashvisor, serve as core engines for this entire analysis process. These platforms are designed to simplify complex calculations while integrating real-world data into your investment decisions. DealCheck allows you to quickly analyze cash flow, expenses, financing structures, and ROI scenarios, while Mashvisor provides deeper insights into rental market trends, occupancy rates, and property performance across different strategies such as short-term and long-term rentals. When combined with AI tools like ChatGPT, these platforms create a powerful ecosystem where analysis becomes both fast and highly accurate. You are no longer switching between spreadsheets, reports, and manual calculations—you are operating within a unified intelligence system. As you move deeper into this book, you will begin to understand that the true power of AI in property analysis is not just speed, but clarity. Many investors fail not because they lack opportunities, but because they cannot clearly see which opportunities are truly profitable. AI eliminates this confusion by presenting data in a structured and actionable format. It highlights strengths and weaknesses of each deal, identifies hidden costs, projects realistic outcomes, and helps you understand the long-term implications of your decisions. This clarity is what allows you to move faster in competitive markets without increasing your level of risk.

It is also important to understand that AI does not replace investor judgment—it enhances it. The most successful investors will always be those who combine technology with experience and intuition. AI provides the analytical foundation, but you are still the decision-maker. You determine strategy, risk tolerance, and long-term goals. What AI does is remove uncertainty from the equation, allowing you to focus on strategy rather than calculations. This shift is what allows investors to scale from individual deals to full portfolios with confidence.

Throughout this book, you will also begin to see how property analysis connects directly to all other areas of real estate investing. Deal evaluation is not an isolated step; it is the bridge between deal sourcing and deal execution. Without accurate analysis, even the best leads can become bad investments. With AI-powered analysis, even average deals can be transformed into strategic opportunities when structured correctly. This interconnected system is what allows modern investors to operate at a much higher level of efficiency than ever before.

Ultimately, Book 3 is about building a new mindset around real estate investing—one that is rooted in data, precision, and intelligence rather than intuition alone. It is about learning to trust systems that process more information than any human could handle manually, while still maintaining control over your investment decisions. It is about removing fear, reducing uncertainty, and replacing hesitation with clarity. Once you master AI-driven property analysis and deal evaluation, you are no longer guessing your way through real estate. You are operating with a structured framework that allows you to consistently identify strong opportunities, avoid high-risk mistakes, and build long-term wealth with confidence and control.

Chapter 1

# The Foundation of AI Property Analysis and Why It Changes Everything

Real estate investing has always been defined by one core challenge: uncertainty. Every decision, from purchasing a property to estimating its value after repairs, has historically required a combination of experience, instinct, and incomplete data. Investors would look at comparable sales, review rental listings, estimate expenses, and then make their best educated guess. Even seasoned professionals would admit that no matter how refined their process became, there was always an element of risk that could not be fully eliminated. This is where AI property analysis fundamentally changes the game. Instead of relying on fragmented information and subjective interpretation, artificial intelligence brings structure, speed, and predictive accuracy to every layer of deal evaluation.

At its core, AI property analysis is about transforming raw data into actionable intelligence. A single property is not just a building; it is a dynamic financial system influenced by hundreds of variables including location trends, interest rates, rental demand, neighborhood development, economic cycles, and buyer behavior. In the past, analyzing all of these factors required manual effort and access to multiple tools that did not communicate with each other. Today, AI systems are capable of aggregating, interpreting, and synthesizing this information in seconds. This allows investors to see the true potential of a property before making any financial commitment.

One of the most important shifts that AI introduces is the transition from static analysis to dynamic forecasting. Traditional spreadsheets provide a snapshot in time, but real estate markets are constantly evolving. Rental rates change, demand fluctuates, interest rates rise or fall, and neighborhood conditions improve or decline. AI models continuously update their analysis based on real-time data feeds, which means the investor is no longer working with outdated assumptions. Instead, they are working with living models that adapt as conditions change. This creates a far more accurate understanding of cash flow potential, appreciation trends, and overall investment viability.

Another foundational element of AI property analysis is its ability to standardize deal evaluation. One of the biggest challenges in real estate investing is inconsistency. Two investors can look at the same property and arrive at completely different conclusions based on their personal experience or bias. AI eliminates this inconsistency by applying uniform evaluation criteria across all properties.

Metrics such as cash-on-cash return, net operating income, internal rate of return, and risk exposure are calculated using standardized formulas that remove emotional influence. This creates a level playing field where every deal is judged by the same objective criteria.

Cash flow analysis is one of the most critical components of this system. In traditional investing, cash flow is often estimated using rough assumptions about rent, expenses, and financing. However, AI takes this process several steps further by incorporating hyper-local data, historical performance trends, and predictive rental models. Instead of simply asking "What can this property rent for today?", AI asks "What will this property realistically generate in income over the next 1, 3, and 5 years based on market behavior?" This long-term perspective allows investors to avoid short-term traps and focus on sustainable wealth-building opportunities.

Risk assessment is another area where AI delivers a significant advantage. Every investment carries risk, but not all risks are equal. Some properties may have strong cash flow but high maintenance costs. Others may be located in volatile markets with unpredictable appreciation trends. AI assigns structured risk scores based on multiple variables including vacancy probability, repair volatility, financing exposure, and market stability. This allows investors to compare deals not just by profit potential, but by risk-adjusted return. Over time, this leads to a more balanced and resilient portfolio. Another powerful capability of AI property analysis is its ability to simulate multiple investment scenarios. Instead of evaluating a property under a single assumption set, investors can explore different outcomes based on changes in interest rates, rental income, or renovation costs. For example, an investor can instantly see how a property performs if rent increases by 10%, or how cash flow is impacted if financing costs rise. This level of scenario modeling was previously reserved for large institutional investors, but AI makes it accessible to individual investors operating from anywhere in the world.

AI also plays a critical role in eliminating information overload. In real estate, there is no shortage of data, but much of it is unstructured and difficult to interpret. MLS listings, rental platforms, tax records, market reports, and neighborhood statistics all contain valuable insights, but manually processing them is time-consuming and inefficient. AI consolidates these data sources into a single analytical framework, filtering out irrelevant information and highlighting what truly matters. This allows investors to focus on decision-making rather than data collection.

The integration of tools like DealCheck and Mashvisor represents the practical application of these concepts.

DealCheck simplifies financial modeling by allowing investors to quickly input property details and generate comprehensive analysis reports. Mashvisor expands this capability by incorporating rental market intelligence, occupancy trends, and short-term rental performance data. When combined with AI-driven interpretation, these tools become far more powerful than standalone calculators. They become decision engines that guide investors toward optimal outcomes.

As investors begin to adopt AI property analysis, they also experience a psychological shift. Instead of feeling overwhelmed by uncertainty, they begin to feel in control of complexity. The fear of making a bad investment is replaced by confidence in data-driven decision-making. This shift is subtle but extremely powerful because it directly impacts behavior. Investors become more disciplined, more strategic, and more willing to act quickly when opportunities arise because they trust the system guiding their decisions.

It is also important to understand that AI does not eliminate the need for human judgment. Rather, it enhances it. AI provides structure, but investors still define strategy. AI calculates probabilities, but investors choose direction. This partnership between human intuition and machine intelligence is what creates the most powerful investment outcomes. The investor becomes less of a calculator and more of a strategist, focusing on long-term wealth building instead of manual analysis. Ultimately, this chapter establishes the foundation for everything that follows in AI Property Analysis & Deal Evaluation. Without understanding how AI processes data, evaluates risk, and forecasts outcomes, it is impossible to fully leverage its power in real-world investing. Once this foundation is in place, every subsequent tool, strategy, and framework becomes significantly more effective because it is built on a system of clarity rather than guesswork. The future of real estate investing belongs to those who can combine speed, data, and strategic thinking—and AI is the engine that makes that possible.

### *The Investor Who Stopped Guessing*

Ethan had been investing in real estate for almost a decade, but he never felt like he had truly mastered it. On the surface, he was successful. He owned several rental properties, had completed a few profitable flips, and generated steady cash flow each month. But behind the scenes, every decision he made carried a quiet sense of uncertainty. He often wondered if he was truly maximizing his returns or simply getting lucky with good timing. Each new deal felt like starting from scratch, and even after years of experience, he still relied heavily on intuition and rough calculations.

One evening, Ethan sat at his kitchen table reviewing a new property deal that had just come across his desk. The numbers looked decent at first glance. The property was in a growing neighborhood, the price seemed reasonable, and rental demand in the area was strong. But as he dug deeper, the same familiar questions began to surface. Were the repair estimates accurate? Was he underestimating vacancy risk? Would the rental income hold steady over the next few years, or was he being overly optimistic? He opened multiple spreadsheets, cross-checked listings, and tried to piece together a clear picture, but the more data he reviewed, the more uncertain he became.

Frustrated, Ethan leaned back in his chair and realized something uncomfortable. After all these years, he was still guessing.

A few weeks later, a colleague introduced him to a new way of analyzing deals using artificial intelligence. At first, Ethan was skeptical. He had seen plenty of tools and software promising to simplify investing, but most of them were just slightly improved calculators. Still, he decided to give it a chance. He input the same property he had been struggling with into an AI-powered analysis system.

Within seconds, everything changed.

The screen filled with structured insights he had never seen before. Instead of scattered assumptions, he was looking at a complete financial breakdown. Cash flow projections were displayed across multiple timeframes. Risk factors were clearly ranked and explained. Rental income was modeled based on real-time market data, not just static listings. Even appreciation potential was estimated using historical trends and neighborhood development patterns. What had taken him hours of manual work was now presented in a clear, organized format in less than a minute.

Ethan sat in silence, staring at the results.

For the first time, he wasn't guessing. He was analyzing.

He ran another property through the system. Then another. Each time, the AI revealed patterns he had never considered. Some deals he thought were strong were actually high-risk when adjusted for vacancy and maintenance costs. Others that he had overlooked turned out to have strong long-term cash flow potential that he had completely missed. The system didn't just give him numbers—it gave him perspective.

Over time, Ethan began to notice a shift in how he approached investing. He no longer spent hours second-guessing himself. Instead, he focused on strategy. He began comparing deals based on structured risk scores rather than gut feeling. He stopped chasing properties that "felt right" and started prioritizing those that performed well under multiple scenarios. His confidence didn't come from knowing everything—it came from trusting the system that analyzed everything for him.

Months later, Ethan closed on one of his most profitable deals yet. But what surprised him most wasn't the profit. It was how calm the entire process felt. There was no anxiety, no uncertainty, no internal debate that dragged on for days. He had already seen every angle of the deal before making the decision. He understood the risks, the upside, and the long-term projections with a level of clarity he had never experienced before.

That night, Ethan realized something important. He hadn't just upgraded his tools. He had changed the way he thought.

He was no longer an investor who guessed his way through deals.

He had become an investor who saw clearly before he acted.

*Chapter 2*

# AI Deal Evaluation Systems and the Mechanics of Smarter Investing

Once the foundation of AI property analysis is understood, the next evolution in real estate investing is learning how to apply that intelligence directly to deal evaluation. This is where theory becomes execution. Many investors can identify opportunities and even run basic numbers, but very few have a consistent system for determining whether a deal should actually be pursued, negotiated, or rejected. AI deal evaluation systems solve this problem by creating a structured framework that removes ambiguity and replaces it with repeatable logic. Instead of relying on instinct or fragmented spreadsheets, investors gain access to a unified evaluation process that assesses every deal using consistent financial, market, and risk-based criteria.

At the core of AI deal evaluation is the concept of standardized scoring. Every property, regardless of type or location, can be broken down into measurable components such as income potential, expense structure, financing cost, appreciation trend, and risk exposure. Traditionally, investors would mentally weigh these factors in an unstructured way, often giving more importance to one variable while unintentionally ignoring others. AI eliminates this imbalance by assigning weighted values to each category. This means that a property is no longer judged on a single attractive feature like low price or high rent potential, but instead evaluated holistically across all financial dimensions.

One of the most powerful elements of AI deal evaluation is cash flow modeling. Cash flow is often misunderstood by beginner investors because it is reduced to a simple equation of rent minus mortgage and expenses. However, real cash flow is far more complex. It includes vacancy assumptions, maintenance reserves, management fees, insurance fluctuations, tax variations, and unexpected operational costs. AI systems incorporate all of these variables simultaneously and simulate real-world operating conditions over time. This produces a far more accurate projection of monthly and annual profitability, helping investors avoid deals that appear strong on paper but fail under realistic conditions.

Another essential component is return on investment analysis. ROI is often used as a broad metric, but in AI systems it becomes a multi-layered evaluation. Instead of just calculating basic percentage returns, AI evaluates cash-on-cash return, internal rate of return, equity growth over time, and opportunity cost compared to alternative investments. This allows investors to understand not just how much money a deal can make, but how efficiently it generates returns relative to other opportunities in the market. This level of comparison is critical for scaling portfolios because it ensures capital is always deployed in the most productive way possible.

AI deal evaluation also introduces a deeper level of rental projection accuracy. Instead of relying on generic rental estimates or limited comparable properties, AI pulls from large datasets that include current listings, historical rental performance, seasonal fluctuations, and neighborhood demand patterns. It then adjusts projections based on property condition, size, amenities, and target tenant demographics. This allows investors to understand not only what a property can rent for today, but how stable and sustainable that income will be over time. This long-term perspective is essential for building reliable passive income streams.

Risk analysis is another area where AI fundamentally transforms decision-making. In traditional investing, risk is often subjective and inconsistently applied. One investor may consider a property risky due to location, while another may see it as an opportunity based on price appreciation potential. AI removes this inconsistency by quantifying risk across multiple categories including market volatility, financing sensitivity, tenant stability, maintenance exposure, and liquidity risk. Each deal is assigned a risk profile that allows for direct comparison between properties, making it easier to balance high-return opportunities with stable long-term investments.

A key advantage of AI systems is their ability to run scenario simulations instantly. Instead of analyzing a deal under a single assumption set, investors can explore multiple outcomes. For example, they can see how a property performs if interest rates increase, if rental income drops, or if renovation costs exceed initial estimates. These scenario-based evaluations help investors understand worst-case, best-case, and most-likely outcomes before committing capital. This level of foresight significantly reduces the likelihood of financial surprises after acquisition.

AI also enhances decision speed without sacrificing accuracy. In competitive real estate markets, timing is often as important as analysis. Deals can be lost simply because investors take too long to evaluate them. AI eliminates this delay by automating the most time-consuming parts of analysis. Instead of spending hours gathering data, building spreadsheets, and verifying assumptions, investors can receive a complete deal breakdown in minutes. This allows them to act quickly when high-quality opportunities appear, giving them a significant competitive advantage. Another important aspect of AI deal evaluation is comparative analysis. Investors rarely evaluate just one property at a time. More often, they are choosing between multiple opportunities with different strengths and weaknesses. AI systems allow side-by-side comparisons that highlight which property offers the best combination of cash flow, appreciation potential, and risk-adjusted return. This helps eliminate emotional decision-making and ensures that capital is allocated to the most efficient deal available, not just the most appealing one.

The integration of tools like DealCheck and Mashvisor brings this entire system into practical application. DealCheck allows investors to input property data and immediately receive structured financial reports, while Mashvisor adds market intelligence layers such as rental demand, occupancy trends, and short-term rental performance insights. When combined with AI interpretation, these tools become far more powerful than standalone platforms. They act as the foundation of a decision-making engine that continuously refines investment choices based on evolving data.

As investors begin using AI deal evaluation systems consistently, they experience a noticeable shift in their decision-making behavior. Instead of chasing deals based on emotion or urgency, they begin to operate with discipline and structure. They learn to walk away from properties that do not meet their criteria, even if they initially appear attractive. This discipline is one of the most important factors in long-term success because it prevents capital from being tied up in low-performing assets.

Over time, AI deal evaluation also improves investor intuition. While it may seem counterintuitive, relying on data-driven systems actually strengthens judgment rather than replacing it. As investors review more AI-generated insights, they begin to recognize patterns in successful deals. They start to understand which combinations of factors consistently produce strong returns and which signals indicate hidden risks. This creates a feedback loop where human experience and machine intelligence reinforce each other.

Ultimately, AI deal evaluation systems represent a shift from reactive investing to proactive strategy. Instead of responding to opportunities as they appear, investors begin to filter and shape opportunities based on clearly defined criteria. They stop asking "Is this a good deal?" and start asking "Does this deal fit my strategy?" This subtle but powerful change transforms investing from a series of isolated decisions into a structured, scalable system for wealth creation.

### *The Day Marcus Stopped Trusting Gut Feeling*

Marcus had always considered himself a "natural" when it came to real estate investing. He didn't rely heavily on spreadsheets or complex analysis. Instead, he trusted his instincts. If a property felt right, he moved quickly. If something felt off, he walked away. For years, this approach worked well enough to keep him profitable, and he took pride in his ability to make fast decisions while others hesitated.

But over time, the market began to change. Deals became more competitive, data became more accessible, and other investors started using advanced tools to evaluate properties faster and more accurately than he could. Marcus noticed that even though he was still closing deals, his margins were shrinking. He was buying properties that looked good on the surface, but some of them were underperforming once they were fully stabilized. Expenses were higher than expected. Vacancy periods were longer. Renovation costs kept creeping upward.

One evening, Marcus reviewed his portfolio and felt a growing sense of frustration. He had spent years building his system, but something wasn't working anymore. He realized that his "gut feeling" approach wasn't evolving with the market. It had worked in a simpler environment, but now he was competing against investors who were using data at a level he could not match manually.

A colleague eventually introduced him to an AI-based deal evaluation platform. Marcus was skeptical. He had seen software tools before, but they always felt like complicated calculators that still required too much manual input. Still, he agreed to test it on a deal he was currently analyzing—a small multi-family property in a growing suburban area.

He entered the basic information: purchase price, estimated rent, square footage, and general expenses. Within moments, the system generated a full evaluation report. At first, Marcus skimmed it quickly, expecting the same basic breakdown he was used to seeing. But as he looked deeper, he realized this was different.

The system didn't just show him cash flow. It showed variability. It modeled what would happen if rents dropped by 5%, 10%, or 15%. It calculated how long he could sustain negative cash flow before breaking even reserves were exhausted. It even highlighted potential maintenance risks based on the age of major systems in the property and comparable data from similar buildings in the area.

Then came the risk score.

The property, which had initially felt like a solid "yes" to Marcus, was labeled as moderate-to-high risk due to rising insurance costs and fluctuating rental demand in the specific sub-market. That single insight stopped him cold. He had completely overlooked those factors. Curious, Marcus ran another property through the system. Then another. Each time, the results challenged his assumptions. Deals he thought were safe revealed hidden risks. Properties he had dismissed showed surprisingly strong long-term performance when analyzed under multiple scenarios.

For the first time in years, Marcus wasn't relying on instinct. He was seeing the full picture.

Weeks later, Marcus made a decision that surprised even himself. He passed on a deal he would have normally purchased without hesitation. The property looked good, the location was strong, and the numbers seemed acceptable. But the AI system showed a different reality. High maintenance exposure, lower-than-expected rental stability, and unfavorable financing sensitivity made it a weaker investment than alternatives in his pipeline.

Instead of feeling regret, Marcus felt clarity.

A few months later, he closed on a different property that the AI system had ranked significantly higher. This time, everything went according to plan. Cash flow matched projections. Expenses stayed within range. Tenant demand remained strong. For the first time, Marcus didn't feel like he had gotten lucky. He felt like he had made a calculated decision backed by a system that consistently removed uncertainty from the equation. Sitting in his office after closing, Marcus reflected on how much had changed. He was still the decision-maker, still the investor, still responsible for every outcome. But now, he wasn't operating in the dark. He had transitioned from guessing to evaluating, from reacting to analyzing, from instinct to intelligence.

And that shift changed everything about the way he invested from that moment forward.

*Chapter 3*

# AI Cash Flow Intelligence and Predictive Investment Performance

At the heart of every real estate investment decision lies one unavoidable truth: cash flow determines survival. Appreciation, equity growth, and tax advantages may enhance long-term wealth, but cash flow is what keeps a property sustainable month after month. Without reliable cash flow, even appreciating assets can become financial burdens. This is why AI-driven cash flow intelligence represents one of the most transformative advancements in modern real estate investing. Instead of treating cash flow as a simple static calculation, AI redefines it as a dynamic, predictive system that reflects real-world complexity, market behavior, and future uncertainty.

Traditional cash flow analysis is typically built on a basic formula: rental income minus expenses equals profit. While this approach is simple, it is also dangerously incomplete. It assumes stability in variables that are constantly changing. Rents fluctuate, vacancies occur, repairs emerge unexpectedly, and financing conditions shift over time. Most importantly, it fails to account for long-term variability in market cycles. AI systems correct this by transforming cash flow analysis into a forward-looking model that simulates performance under multiple real-world conditions, rather than relying on a single static snapshot.

One of the most powerful capabilities of AI cash flow intelligence is multi-layer forecasting. Instead of calculating a single monthly profit number, AI generates a range of outcomes based on different assumptions. It evaluates best-case scenarios where rental income increases and expenses remain stable, base-case scenarios where conditions remain average, and worst-case scenarios where vacancies rise or costs increase. This allows investors to see not just how much a property can make, but how it behaves under stress. This stress-testing function is critical because it reveals whether a deal is truly resilient or only profitable under ideal conditions.

Another key advancement is the integration of real-time expense modeling. In traditional investing, expenses are often underestimated or generalized based on outdated benchmarks. AI systems, however, analyze actual property characteristics, local insurance trends, tax histories, maintenance data, and utility cost patterns to generate far more accurate expense projections. This includes long-term capital expenditure forecasting, which accounts for major future costs such as roof replacement, HVAC systems, plumbing, and structural repairs.

By incorporating these elements into cash flow projections, AI ensures that investors are not blindsided by hidden costs that could erode profitability over time.

Rental income forecasting is also significantly enhanced through AI-driven systems. Instead of relying solely on comparable properties or listing averages, AI evaluates rental demand trends, tenant demographics, seasonal patterns, and neighborhood economic indicators. It then projects rental income trajectories over time, allowing investors to understand whether rents are likely to grow, stagnate, or decline. This predictive insight is essential for long-term planning because it determines whether a property will improve in value or become stagnant in performance.

A critical component of AI cash flow intelligence is time-based projection modeling. Traditional analysis often focuses on Year 1 performance, but real estate investing is a long-term game. AI expands the analysis horizon to include multi-year projections that simulate how cash flow evolves over time. This includes mortgage amortization effects, rent growth compounding, expense inflation, and refinancing opportunities. By viewing cash flow as a timeline rather than a single point, investors can better understand how wealth accumulates and how equity can be strategically leveraged in the future.

Another major advantage of AI systems is sensitivity analysis. This process identifies which variables have the greatest impact on cash flow performance. For example, a property may be highly sensitive to vacancy rates but relatively stable in terms of maintenance costs. Another may be heavily affected by interest rate changes but less impacted by rental fluctuations. Understanding these sensitivities allows investors to make more informed decisions about risk exposure and financing strategies. It also helps them structure deals in ways that minimize downside risk while preserving upside potential.

AI cash flow systems also introduce the concept of comparative performance ranking. Instead of evaluating properties in isolation, investors can compare multiple deals side by side based on standardized performance metrics. These metrics include net operating income, cash-on-cash return, debt coverage ratio, and long-term equity growth potential. This allows investors to identify not just profitable deals, but the most efficient allocation of capital across their entire portfolio. Over time, this leads to more optimized investment decisions and higher overall returns.

Another important feature is automated scenario adjustment. As market conditions change, AI systems can update projections dynamically. If interest rates rise, the system recalculates mortgage impact on cash flow. If rental demand shifts in a specific area, projections adjust accordingly. This continuous recalibration ensures that investors are always working with current and relevant data rather than outdated assumptions. It transforms cash flow analysis from a one-time calculation into an ongoing intelligence system.

The integration of AI tools like ChatGPT with financial modeling platforms such as DealCheck and Mashvisor further enhances this process. ChatGPT can interpret data patterns, explain financial implications in simple language, and identify hidden risks that may not be obvious in raw numbers. Meanwhile, DealCheck provides structured financial modeling, and Mashvisor adds deep market intelligence and rental analytics. When combined, these tools create a full ecosystem where cash flow analysis becomes both highly technical and easily understandable.

One of the most overlooked benefits of AI cash flow intelligence is decision confidence. Many investors hesitate not because they lack opportunities, but because they are uncertain about outcomes. AI reduces this uncertainty by providing structured probability-based insights. Instead of asking "Will this property perform well?", investors can see "This property has an 82% probability of maintaining positive cash flow under current market conditions." This shift from ambiguity to probability allows for faster and more confident decision-making. As investors begin using AI cash flow systems consistently, they also begin to change how they think about risk. Instead of viewing risk as something to avoid entirely, they begin to see it as something that can be measured, managed, and optimized. High-risk properties may still be attractive if they offer strong upside potential, while low-risk properties may be preferred for portfolio stability. This nuanced understanding allows for more strategic portfolio construction that balances growth and security.

Ultimately, AI cash flow intelligence represents a shift from reactive investing to predictive investing. Instead of waiting to see how a property performs after purchase, investors can simulate its performance before acquisition with a high degree of accuracy. This fundamentally changes the decision-making process. It allows investors to filter out weak opportunities early, focus only on high-quality deals, and scale their portfolios with significantly lower uncertainty.

Once this system is fully understood and implemented, cash flow is no longer something that surprises an investor after purchase. It becomes something that is fully mapped, understood, and projected before the deal is ever executed. This is the true power of AI-driven real estate investing: turning uncertainty into structured, predictable financial intelligence.

## *The Investor Who Learned to See the Future of Cash Flow*

Daniel had been investing in rental properties for years, and on paper, he looked successful. He owned several single-family homes and a few small multifamily units that generated steady monthly income. But despite his experience, Daniel always felt like he was reacting to problems rather than predicting them. Some months his properties performed well, and other months unexpected expenses or vacancies would eat into his profits. He never felt fully in control of his portfolio's financial performance.

One evening, after reviewing yet another disappointing quarterly report, Daniel realized something uncomfortable. He didn't actually understand his own cash flow in a meaningful way. He understood what had happened in the past, but he had no clear visibility into what might happen in the future. Every projection he made was based on assumptions that often turned out to be slightly wrong. It wasn't that his properties were bad—it was that his analysis was incomplete.

A fellow investor introduced him to an AI-based cash flow forecasting system. At first, Daniel dismissed it as just another calculator with a modern interface. He had seen dozens of tools like that before. But after some hesitation, he decided to test it using one of his existing properties—a duplex he had owned for three years. He entered the property details into the system and waited.

Within moments, the screen filled with structured projections that immediately caught his attention. Instead of showing a single monthly cash flow number, the system displayed multiple scenarios. One scenario showed strong positive cash flow under stable conditions. Another showed moderate performance with increased vacancy rates. A third scenario revealed what would happen if interest rates rose and rental growth slowed.

For the first time, Daniel wasn't looking at a single answer. He was looking at possibilities.

Curious, he dug deeper. The system highlighted upcoming expense risks he had not fully accounted for, including roof maintenance and HVAC replacement within the next few years. It also showed that while the property was currently profitable, its sensitivity to rental fluctuations was higher than he had realized. A small drop in rent would significantly impact his monthly cash flow.

Daniel sat back in his chair, surprised. He had owned this property for years and had never seen it this clearly.

Over the next few weeks, Daniel began analyzing all of his properties through the system. The results were eye-opening.

Some properties he considered strong performers were actually vulnerable to expense spikes. Others he had overlooked showed surprisingly stable long-term performance when modeled over multiple years. One property that had always been "just okay" turned out to be one of his most resilient assets when viewed through long-term cash flow projections.

The real shift came when Daniel evaluated a new deal. In the past, he would have made a quick judgment based on rent estimates and mortgage payments. This time, he ran it through the AI system. The results showed strong initial cash flow, but also revealed high sensitivity to vacancy risk and rising insurance costs. The system projected that over a five-year period, the property would likely underperform compared to other available opportunities.

For the first time, Daniel walked away from a deal not because of hesitation, but because of clarity.

Months later, Daniel looked back at his portfolio and noticed something different. His decisions had become more deliberate. His cash flow was more stable. And most importantly, he was no longer surprised by his financial outcomes. He had shifted from reacting to predicting.

Sitting in his office late one night, Daniel reviewed his updated projections across all properties. Instead of uncertainty, he saw patterns. Instead of surprises, he saw forecasts. Instead of risk he couldn't understand, he saw risk he could measure.

And in that moment, Daniel realized something powerful.

He hadn't just improved his investing.

He had learned how to see his financial future before it happened.

*Chapter 4*

# AI Risk Scoring and Intelligent Deal Filtering

In real estate investing, risk is not something that can be eliminated—it is something that must be understood, measured, and controlled. Every property carries a different combination of risks, whether those risks are related to market conditions, tenant stability, financing structure, physical condition, or long-term appreciation potential. The difference between successful investors and struggling investors is not that one avoids risk entirely, but that one understands risk with far greater clarity. AI risk scoring systems fundamentally change how investors perceive and manage uncertainty by turning what was once subjective judgment into structured, data-driven intelligence.

Traditional risk evaluation in real estate has always been inconsistent. One investor may view a property as safe because it is located in a growing neighborhood, while another may consider it risky due to high purchase price or potential maintenance costs. These opinions are often based on experience, intuition, or incomplete information. As a result, risk becomes something emotional rather than analytical. AI eliminates this inconsistency by assigning quantifiable risk scores to every deal based on a wide range of measurable variables. Instead of asking whether a deal "feels safe," investors can now see exactly how risky it is across multiple categories.

AI risk scoring works by breaking a property down into core risk components and analyzing each one independently. Market risk evaluates the stability and growth potential of the surrounding area. Financial risk measures the impact of financing structure, interest rates, and leverage levels. Operational risk examines ongoing property management factors such as maintenance, tenant turnover, and vacancy likelihood. Physical risk evaluates the condition of the property itself, including age of systems, required repairs, and structural integrity. When combined, these categories create a comprehensive risk profile that reflects the true investment exposure.

One of the most powerful aspects of AI risk scoring is its ability to normalize risk across different property types. A single-family rental, a multifamily building, and a short-term rental all carry different types of risk, making direct comparison difficult in traditional analysis. AI solves this problem by converting all risk factors into a standardized scoring system. This allows investors to compare completely different properties on equal terms. Instead of relying on intuition to decide between a stable low-yield property and a higher-yield but riskier investment, investors can see a clear, structured comparison of risk-adjusted returns.

Another key advantage of AI risk scoring is predictive risk modeling. Traditional analysis focuses on current conditions, but AI evaluates how risk changes over time. For example, a property in a rapidly developing area may appear low risk today but could become higher risk if market saturation increases or rental demand shifts. Similarly, a property with aging systems may appear stable now but carry increasing risk over the next five to ten years due to rising maintenance costs. AI captures these future dynamics by analyzing historical trends, local development patterns, and economic indicators.

Financial risk is another critical area where AI provides deep insight. Many investors underestimate how sensitive a property is to changes in interest rates, financing terms, or leverage levels. AI systems simulate different financial environments to determine how stable a property remains under varying conditions. For example, a deal that looks profitable under current interest rates may become cash-flow negative if rates increase slightly. By identifying this sensitivity early, investors can avoid deals that are overly dependent on favorable financing conditions.

Operational risk analysis is equally important because it reflects the day-to-day reality of managing a property. AI evaluates tenant turnover rates, historical vacancy patterns, maintenance frequency, and management complexity. Properties that require frequent repairs or attract unstable tenant profiles are assigned higher operational risk scores. This helps investors understand not just how profitable a property might be, but how demanding it will be to maintain. In many cases, operational risk becomes the hidden factor that determines whether a property remains profitable long term.

Market risk evaluation adds another layer of intelligence by analyzing macro and microeconomic trends. AI systems assess job growth, population shifts, local infrastructure development, and rental demand trends. A property located in a growing job market with increasing population density will typically receive a lower market risk score, while properties in stagnant or declining areas will show higher risk exposure. This allows investors to align their portfolios with long-term growth markets rather than short-term fluctuations.

One of the most valuable outcomes of AI risk scoring is deal filtering. Instead of manually reviewing dozens of properties and trying to determine which ones are worth deeper analysis, investors can use AI to automatically filter out high-risk or low-quality deals at the earliest stage. This saves significant time and allows investors to focus only on opportunities that meet their specific risk tolerance and investment strategy. Over time, this filtering process becomes a powerful system for scaling investment activity efficiently.

AI also introduces the concept of risk-adjusted decision-making. Instead of evaluating properties based solely on potential returns, investors begin to evaluate how much return they are receiving relative to the level of risk involved. A property with moderate returns but low risk may be more attractive than a high-return property with unstable fundamentals. This shift in thinking leads to more balanced portfolios and reduces exposure to catastrophic losses.

Integration with tools like DealCheck, Mashvisor, and AI-driven models like ChatGPT further enhances risk analysis by adding context and interpretation. DealCheck provides structured financial data, Mashvisor offers market and rental insights, and AI systems interpret these inputs to produce a unified risk profile. This layered approach ensures that risk evaluation is not based on a single data source, but on a combination of financial, market, and behavioral intelligence.

As investors begin to rely more heavily on AI risk scoring, their behavior changes significantly. They become more selective, more disciplined, and more focused on long-term stability rather than short-term excitement. They begin to understand that not all profitable deals are good deals, and not all high-return opportunities are worth pursuing. This refined decision-making process leads to stronger portfolios and fewer unexpected losses.

Ultimately, AI risk scoring transforms real estate investing from a reactive process into a controlled system of decision-making. Instead of discovering risk after a property is purchased, investors can identify and quantify risk before committing capital. This shift fundamentally changes the nature of investing, turning it from a speculative activity into a structured, data-driven strategy for wealth creation.

*The Deal That Almost Broke Evan*

Evan had always considered himself a confident investor. He liked to move quickly, trust his instincts, and act on opportunities before others could react. Over the years, this approach had brought him both wins and losses, but he believed that speed was his advantage. In competitive markets, hesitation often meant missing out, and Evan prided himself on being decisive.

One afternoon, Evan came across a multifamily property that immediately caught his attention. The price was attractive, the location was decent, and the projected rental income looked strong. On the surface, it seemed like exactly the kind of deal he liked—simple, straightforward, and profitable. Without overthinking, he began running basic numbers in his head. Cash flow looked positive. The neighborhood was stable. Demand for rentals in the area was solid.

For Evan, that was usually enough.

But this time, something felt slightly different. A colleague had recently introduced him to an AI-based risk scoring system and encouraged him to run his deals through it before making decisions. Evan wasn't fully convinced yet, but he agreed to try it on this particular property just out of curiosity.

He entered the data into the system and waited.

At first, the results seemed similar to his own assumptions. The property showed moderate returns and acceptable cash flow. But then the risk analysis appeared.

Evan paused.

The system assigned the property a higher-than-expected risk score. Market risk was flagged due to slowing population growth in the area. Operational risk was elevated because of historical tenant turnover patterns in similar buildings nearby. Financial risk showed sensitivity to interest rate increases that could quickly turn positive cash flow into negative territory.

Physical risk was also noted due to the age of major systems in the building. Evan frowned. None of this had been obvious from his initial review.

Curious, he dug deeper into the breakdown. The AI didn't just give him a score—it explained why. It showed that while current rental demand looked strong, it was heavily seasonal and had fluctuated significantly over the past five years. It also highlighted that recent insurance increases in the region could materially impact long-term cash flow stability. Finally, it modeled what would happen if vacancy rates increased by just a small percentage—and the results were concerning.

Evan leaned back in his chair. For the first time, he realized he wasn't looking at a simple good or bad deal. He was looking at a complex risk profile that he had completely missed.

Still, part of him resisted. He had seen deals like this before succeed, and he didn't want to overthink it. But something about the clarity of the AI breakdown stayed with him.

Over the next few days, Evan ran several other properties through the system. Each time, he noticed patterns he hadn't considered before. Some properties that looked strong on paper carried hidden risks. Others that seemed average were actually more stable than expected. Slowly, his confidence shifted—not away from investing, but away from blind decision-making.

The turning point came when he revisited the original property. After reviewing the AI risk profile again, he made a difficult decision.

He walked away.

A few weeks later, Evan heard from another investor who had purchased a similar property in the same area. At first, the deal seemed fine, but soon after closing, unexpected insurance increases and higher-than-anticipated maintenance costs began eroding cash flow. Vacancy rates also started to rise as local demand softened.

Evan felt a quiet sense of relief.

That property could have easily been his.

Months later, Evan reflected on how much his approach had changed. He still valued speed and decisiveness, but now those traits were balanced with structured analysis. He no longer relied solely on instinct. Instead, he used data to confirm or challenge his assumptions before acting.

Sitting at his desk one evening, Evan looked at his updated pipeline of deals. Each one had a clear risk profile, a structured score, and a detailed breakdown of strengths and weaknesses. Instead of uncertainty, he saw clarity. Instead of guesswork, he saw systems. And for the first time in his investing career, Evan understood something fundamental.

The best deals were not the ones that looked good the fastest.

They were the ones that survived being fully analyzed.

Chapter 5

# AI Deal Filtering Systems and High-Speed Investment Decision Making

In modern real estate investing, the greatest constraint is no longer access to deals—it is the ability to process them efficiently. Investors today are exposed to more opportunities than ever before through MLS platforms, off-market data providers, wholesaler networks, direct marketing campaigns, and AI-generated lead sources. While this abundance of data creates opportunity, it also creates overload. The real challenge is not finding deals, but filtering through them quickly enough to identify the few that are truly worth pursuing. This is where AI deal filtering systems become essential. They transform the chaotic flow of incoming opportunities into a structured, prioritized pipeline of actionable investments.

Traditional deal screening methods are slow and inconsistent. Investors often rely on manual spreadsheets, rough mental calculations, or basic rule-of-thumb criteria such as price per square foot or estimated rent. While these methods can eliminate obviously bad deals, they are not precise enough to handle large volumes of opportunities. As a result, many investors either spend too much time analyzing low-quality deals or miss high-quality opportunities due to inefficiency. AI deal filtering solves this problem by acting as an automated intelligence layer that evaluates every opportunity instantly based on predefined investment criteria.

At the core of AI filtering systems is the concept of rule-based intelligence combined with adaptive learning. Investors define their investment parameters—such as minimum cash flow, acceptable risk level, target ROI, preferred property type, and geographic focus—and the AI system continuously screens incoming deals against these criteria. Unlike static filters, however, AI systems evolve over time by learning from investor behavior and past decisions. If an investor consistently accepts deals with slightly lower cash flow but higher appreciation potential, the system adjusts its weighting accordingly. This creates a personalized filtering engine that aligns with individual investment strategy.

One of the most powerful functions of AI deal filtering is deal prioritization. Instead of presenting investors with an unorganized list of properties, AI ranks opportunities based on overall investment quality. This ranking is not based on a single metric but on a composite score that includes cash flow strength, risk exposure, market growth potential, and financing efficiency. The result is a clear hierarchy of opportunities, allowing investors to immediately focus on the top-tier deals without wasting time on lower-quality options.

Speed is another critical advantage of AI filtering systems. In competitive real estate markets, timing often determines success or failure. High-quality deals are frequently claimed within hours or even minutes of being listed. AI systems dramatically reduce evaluation time by automating the entire initial screening process. Instead of spending hours reviewing each property, investors receive pre-analyzed deals that already meet baseline investment criteria. This allows them to act faster than competitors who are still manually reviewing data.

Another key feature is intelligent deal categorization. AI systems do not simply accept or reject deals—they classify them into strategic categories such as "high cash flow," "value-add opportunity," "long-term appreciation," or "high-risk/high-reward." This categorization helps investors build diversified portfolios by ensuring they are not overexposed to a single investment strategy. It also allows for more strategic capital allocation, where different types of deals serve different roles within an overall investment plan.

AI deal filtering also integrates deeply with predictive analytics. Instead of evaluating deals solely based on current conditions, AI systems forecast how each property is likely to perform over time. This includes projected rent growth, expense escalation, market appreciation, and financing impact. By incorporating forward-looking data, AI ensures that filtered deals are not only good today but remain strong investments in the future. This long-term perspective is critical for building sustainable wealth rather than short-term gains.

Another important function is anomaly detection. AI systems are capable of identifying deals that appear attractive on the surface but contain hidden risks or inconsistencies. For example, a property may show unusually high rental income compared to similar properties in the area. While this might seem like a strong opportunity, AI may flag it as an outlier that requires deeper investigation. Similarly, properties with unusually low expenses or unrealistic projections are flagged for further review. This helps investors avoid misleading listings and reduces exposure to inaccurate data.

AI filtering systems also improve deal sourcing efficiency by integrating directly with lead generation platforms. Instead of manually searching through listings or waiting for deals to appear, investors can receive continuously updated streams of filtered opportunities based on their criteria. This creates a proactive investment system where high-quality deals are delivered automatically rather than manually discovered. Over time, this significantly increases deal flow while reducing time spent on low-value analysis. Another key benefit is emotional neutrality. One of the biggest challenges in real estate investing is emotional decision-making. Investors often become attached to certain deals due to perceived potential, urgency, or external pressure from wholesalers or agents. AI filtering removes this emotional bias by applying consistent, objective criteria to every opportunity. This ensures that decisions are based on data rather than excitement or fear of missing out.

Integration with tools like ChatGPT, PropertyRadar, and PropStream enhances the effectiveness of AI filtering systems. PropertyRadar and PropStream provide raw lead data, including off-market properties, ownership details, and property characteristics. AI systems then process this data, evaluate it against investor criteria, and prioritize the most promising opportunities. ChatGPT adds an interpretive layer by explaining why certain deals are ranked higher, identifying risks, and suggesting strategic actions. Together, these tools create a seamless workflow from data collection to decision execution.

As investors adopt AI deal filtering systems, they experience a significant shift in productivity. Instead of spending hours or days analyzing deals manually, they can evaluate entire pipelines in minutes. This frees up time for higher-level strategic activities such as negotiation, portfolio planning, and capital allocation. It also increases confidence in decision-making because every deal has already been pre-vetted by a structured system. Over time, AI filtering systems also improve investor discipline. By consistently presenting only high-quality opportunities, they reduce the temptation to pursue marginal or emotional deals. Investors begin to trust the system's ranking logic and become more selective in their decision-making. This leads to stronger portfolios with higher average performance and lower risk exposure.

Ultimately, AI deal filtering represents a shift from manual searching to automated intelligence. Instead of working harder to find deals, investors work smarter by allowing systems to identify and prioritize opportunities for them. This transformation is not just about efficiency—it is about fundamentally changing how investment decisions are made. It turns real estate investing from a reactive process into a continuously optimized system for wealth creation.

*The Investor Who Stopped Searching and Started Selecting*

Jason had always believed that success in real estate came from hard work and persistence. Every morning, he would wake up early, open multiple listing platforms, scroll through hundreds of properties, and manually review deal after deal. He took pride in his effort, believing that the more properties he reviewed, the better his chances of finding a great investment. But over time, something began to change. The number of available deals increased, but his ability to process them did not. He was spending more time than ever analyzing opportunities, yet he felt like he was missing the best ones.

One afternoon, after spending nearly five hours reviewing listings, Jason realized he had only properly analyzed a handful of properties. The rest had been skimmed or ignored due to time constraints. He felt overwhelmed. It wasn't that opportunities were lacking—it was that there were too many to properly evaluate. For the first time, Jason understood that his problem was not sourcing deals, but filtering them.

A colleague introduced him to an AI deal filtering system designed to automatically evaluate and rank real estate opportunities. Jason was skeptical at first. He had always trusted his own judgment and wasn't convinced that software could understand real estate better than experience. But curiosity got the better of him, and he decided to test it.

He set up his investment criteria: minimum cash flow requirements, acceptable risk levels, preferred property types, and target ROI thresholds. Then he connected the system to his deal sources and waited.

Within minutes, his entire pipeline transformed.

Instead of a long, unorganized list of properties, Jason now saw a ranked dashboard of filtered opportunities. At the top were a few high-quality deals that matched his criteria almost perfectly. Below them were moderate opportunities categorized by strategy. At the bottom were deals automatically flagged as too risky or misaligned with his goals.

Jason clicked on the first deal. The system provided a full breakdown—cash flow projections, risk score, rental stability, appreciation forecast, and financing impact. Everything was already analyzed. What used to take him hours was now presented instantly.

He moved to the next deal. Then the next. Each one was pre-evaluated, structured, and prioritized.

For the first time, Jason wasn't searching for deals. He was selecting from them.

Over the next week, Jason noticed something even more surprising. His decision-making became faster and more confident. Instead of feeling overwhelmed, he felt focused. Instead of chasing every opportunity, he concentrated only on the top-ranked deals. He began closing faster because he was no longer wasting time on low-quality analysis.

One evening, Jason compared his old workflow to his new system. Previously, he would analyze dozens of properties to find one acceptable deal. Now, he reviewed only a handful of pre-filtered opportunities and spent his time deeply evaluating only the best ones. His efficiency had increased dramatically without sacrificing quality.

Months later, Jason looked at his portfolio and saw a noticeable improvement. His average deal quality had increased. His returns were more consistent. And his stress level had decreased significantly. He was no longer racing through endless listings or second-guessing his decisions.

Sitting in his office late one night, Jason reflected on how much had changed. He realized that the biggest shift wasn't in the deals he was finding—it was in how he was finding them.

He had stopped searching blindly.

And started selecting with precision.

*Chapter 6*

# AI Predictive ROI Modeling and Long-Term Wealth Simulation

Real estate investing is often treated as a short-term decision-making process, where investors focus heavily on immediate cash flow, purchase price, and initial repair costs. However, true wealth in real estate is not created in the first month or even the first year of ownership. It is built over time through appreciation, debt reduction, rent growth, tax advantages, and strategic refinancing. This is where AI predictive ROI modeling fundamentally transforms the way investors evaluate opportunities. Instead of asking "What will this property earn today?", AI allows investors to ask a far more powerful question: "What will this property be worth to me over the next 5, 10, or 20 years under different market conditions?"

Traditional ROI calculations are limited because they rely on static assumptions. Investors typically input current rent, current expenses, and current financing terms, then calculate a simple return percentage. While this provides a basic snapshot, it fails to account for the dynamic nature of real estate. Markets change, rents increase, expenses rise, and loan balances decrease over time. AI systems solve this limitation by simulating long-term financial performance using predictive modeling that incorporates historical trends, economic cycles, and property-specific data.

One of the most important aspects of AI predictive ROI modeling is time-based cash flow evolution. Instead of treating cash flow as a fixed number, AI projects how income and expenses will change over time. Rent growth is modeled based on local demand trends, inflation rates, and historical rental increases in the area. Expenses are projected using inflation assumptions, maintenance schedules, and insurance trend data. Financing costs are modeled based on amortization schedules and potential refinancing scenarios. When combined, these factors create a living financial model that evolves year by year.

Another critical component is equity growth simulation. Equity in real estate is not just created through appreciation; it is also built through mortgage paydown and strategic refinancing. AI systems calculate how much equity is being built each year through principal reduction and how that equity can be leveraged for future investments. This allows investors to see not only the value of a single property but its role as a wealth-building engine within a larger portfolio strategy.

Appreciation forecasting is another area where AI delivers significant value. Traditional investors often rely on general market assumptions such as "3% annual appreciation." However, real estate markets are highly localized and influenced by factors such as job growth, infrastructure development, population migration, and zoning changes. AI systems analyze these variables at a granular level to generate more accurate appreciation projections. This helps investors identify markets with strong long-term growth potential rather than relying on broad national averages.

AI predictive ROI models also incorporate refinancing strategies into long-term simulations. Refinancing is one of the most powerful wealth-building tools in real estate, yet it is often overlooked in basic analysis. AI systems simulate scenarios where investors refinance properties at different points in time to extract equity, improve cash flow, or reduce interest expenses. This allows investors to see how strategic refinancing can accelerate portfolio growth and increase overall return on investment.

Another powerful feature is scenario-based ROI comparison. Instead of evaluating a single outcome, AI models multiple future scenarios based on different economic conditions. For example, one scenario may assume stable economic growth, another may simulate a recessionary period, and another may model high inflation conditions. Each scenario produces a different ROI outcome, allowing investors to understand how resilient their investment is under varying macroeconomic environments. This type of stress testing is critical for building portfolios that can withstand market volatility.

AI also introduces the concept of opportunity cost analysis. Every investment decision comes with trade-offs. By choosing one property, an investor is simultaneously choosing not to invest in another. AI systems compare multiple investment options side by side and simulate their long-term performance over identical time horizons. This allows investors to see which deal produces the highest long-term wealth accumulation, not just the highest short-term return. This shift in perspective leads to more strategic capital allocation decisions.

Another key advantage of AI predictive ROI modeling is portfolio-level simulation. Instead of analyzing properties individually, AI systems can model entire portfolios as interconnected financial ecosystems. This includes interactions between cash flow, debt levels, equity accumulation, and reinvestment strategies. Investors can see how their portfolio grows over time, how passive income increases, and how leverage can be strategically used to scale holdings. This transforms investing from a series of isolated decisions into a cohesive wealth-building system. AI also enhances decision confidence by providing probability-weighted outcomes. Instead of presenting a single projected ROI, AI systems display a range of possible outcomes along with likelihood estimates. For example, a property might have a 70% probability of achieving a 12% annual return, a 20% probability of achieving a 15% return, and a 10% probability of underperforming at 8%. This probabilistic approach allows investors to make decisions based on risk-adjusted expectations rather than fixed assumptions.

Integration with tools such as DealCheck, Mashvisor, and AI-driven modeling engines enhances predictive ROI accuracy even further. DealCheck provides structured financial data, Mashvisor adds market intelligence and rental analytics, and AI systems interpret this information to build long-term financial simulations. ChatGPT enhances the experience by explaining projections in simple language, identifying key drivers of return, and helping investors understand complex financial scenarios.

As investors begin using predictive ROI modeling consistently, their mindset shifts significantly. Instead of focusing on immediate gains, they begin to think in terms of long-term wealth trajectories. They start evaluating how each property contributes to their overall financial goals rather than just its standalone performance. This leads to more intentional investing, where every acquisition is part of a larger strategic plan.

Over time, AI predictive ROI modeling also improves investor patience and discipline. Because investors can clearly see long-term outcomes, they are less likely to make impulsive decisions based on short-term market fluctuations. They begin to trust the model's long-term projections and focus on executing strategies that maximize sustained growth rather than short-term excitement.

Ultimately, AI predictive ROI modeling transforms real estate investing from reactive decision-making into forward-looking wealth engineering. It allows investors to see not just what a property is worth today, but what it can become over time under multiple conditions. This shift in perspective is what separates traditional investors from modern AI-driven wealth builders. Instead of chasing deals, they are designing financial futures.

### *The Investor Who Learned to See Ten Years Ahead*

Michael had been investing in real estate for nearly fifteen years. He had built a respectable portfolio of rental properties, flipped several homes, and accumulated steady monthly cash flow. On the surface, he looked successful. But internally,

Michael always felt like he was making decisions one step at a time. He knew what his properties were worth today, but he had no clear understanding of what they would be worth years into the future. Every time he evaluated a new deal, he focused on immediate returns. Cash flow, purchase price, and basic appreciation estimates were his primary tools. He believed that as long as the numbers worked today, the investment was sound. But over time, he noticed something concerning. Some of his best-looking deals had underperformed in the long run, while properties he had almost dismissed ended up becoming some of his strongest assets.

One afternoon, Michael met with a younger investor who approached investing very differently. Instead of talking about monthly cash flow, the investor talked about ten-year projections, equity cycles, refinancing strategies, and long-term wealth modeling. Intrigued, Michael asked how he was able to think so far ahead with such clarity.

The investor introduced him to an AI predictive ROI modeling system.

Michael was skeptical but curious. That evening, he decided to run one of his existing properties through the system. It was a duplex he had owned for four years. He expected to see a slightly more advanced version of his own spreadsheets.

Instead, he saw something entirely different.

The system didn't just show current cash flow. It showed a full ten-year projection. It mapped rent growth year by year, modeled expense inflation, and calculated mortgage paydown over time. It also showed potential refinancing opportunities that could unlock equity and increase cash flow in the future.

Michael stared at the screen in disbelief.

For the first time, he wasn't just seeing what his property was worth now. He was seeing what it could become.

He ran another property. Then another. Each time, the results revealed insights he had never considered. Some properties that looked average today were projected to become strong long-term performers due to rent growth and equity accumulation. Others that were currently profitable showed slowing returns over time due to rising expenses and limited appreciation potential.

The most surprising moment came when he evaluated a property he was considering purchasing. On the surface, it looked like a solid deal with strong monthly cash flow. But the AI model told a different story. Over a ten-year period, rising insurance costs, limited rent growth, and weak appreciation trends significantly reduced its long-term return.

For the first time, Michael paused before making a decision not because he lacked confidence, but because he finally had clarity.

He decided not to purchase the property. Months later, Michael revisited his portfolio using the same system. He began to see patterns he had never noticed before. His strongest-performing assets were not necessarily the ones with the best initial cash flow, but the ones with strong long-term growth trajectories. His weakest assets were those that looked good initially but stagnated over time.

This realization changed everything.

Michael stopped thinking in terms of monthly performance and started thinking in decades. He began structuring his investments around long-term wealth accumulation rather than short-term income. He refinanced strategically, held properties longer when projections showed strong growth, and exited properties when long-term models indicated declining returns.

One evening, Michael looked at his updated portfolio projections. For the first time in his career, he could clearly see where his financial future was heading. It wasn't a guess. It wasn't an estimate. It was a structured projection based on real data and predictive modeling.

Sitting in silence, he realized something profound.

He had spent years investing in real estate.

But only now was he actually seeing the future of his investments.

*Chapter 7*

# AI Portfolio Scaling and Automated Real Estate Wealth Systems

At a certain point in real estate investing, success is no longer determined by individual deals. It becomes a question of systems. The difference between an investor who owns a few profitable properties and one who builds generational wealth is not just experience or capital—it is the ability to scale intelligently. This is where AI portfolio scaling fundamentally changes the game. Instead of managing properties one by one, investors begin operating entire ecosystems of real estate assets that are continuously analyzed, optimized, and improved through artificial intelligence.

Traditional portfolio management is often reactive. Investors review properties periodically, track income and expenses manually, and make adjustments when problems arise. This approach works at small scale but quickly becomes inefficient as the portfolio grows. More properties mean more complexity, more data, more decisions, and more potential for error. AI systems eliminate this bottleneck by transforming portfolio management into a continuous, automated intelligence process. Instead of reacting to problems, investors operate within a system that identifies opportunities and risks in real time.

One of the most important elements of AI portfolio scaling is centralized data integration. In a traditional setup, information is scattered across multiple platforms—bank accounts, property management systems, spreadsheets, rental platforms, and accounting software. This fragmentation makes it difficult to see the full picture. AI solves this by aggregating all data into a unified system that continuously updates and analyzes portfolio performance. Investors can see cash flow, equity growth, occupancy rates, maintenance costs, and debt exposure in one connected environment.

Another critical component is performance optimization across assets. Not all properties in a portfolio perform equally. Some generate strong cash flow, others provide long-term appreciation, and some may underperform due to market conditions or operational inefficiencies. AI systems evaluate each property individually and collectively to determine how it contributes to overall portfolio performance. This allows investors to make strategic decisions such as refinancing underperforming assets, selling low-growth properties, or reinvesting capital into higher-performing opportunities. AI also introduces automated maintenance prediction and operational management. One of the hidden costs in real estate investing is unexpected maintenance and repair expenses. Traditionally, these issues are addressed only after they occur, often causing financial disruption. AI systems analyze property age, historical maintenance data, and comparable asset behavior to predict when major repairs are likely to occur. This allows investors to plan ahead, allocate reserves efficiently, and avoid sudden financial strain. In advanced systems, maintenance alerts can even be automated and integrated with property management workflows.

Another key advantage of AI portfolio scaling is income optimization. Rental income is not static; it can be strategically increased through pricing adjustments, lease structuring, and tenant optimization. AI systems analyze market rent trends, occupancy rates, and tenant behavior to recommend optimal pricing strategies. For example, in high-demand markets, AI may suggest incremental rent increases to maximize income without increasing vacancy risk. In softer markets, it may recommend stability-focused pricing to retain tenants and reduce turnover. This dynamic pricing intelligence helps maximize portfolio-wide revenue efficiency.

Debt management is another area where AI provides significant value. As portfolios scale, leverage becomes a critical factor in growth and risk management. AI systems track loan balances, interest rates, amortization schedules, and refinancing opportunities across all properties. They identify when refinancing could improve cash flow or when debt restructuring could reduce risk exposure. This ensures that capital structure remains optimized at all times, rather than being left static after initial acquisition.

AI portfolio systems also enable strategic scaling decisions. One of the most difficult challenges for investors is knowing when and how to expand. AI addresses this by modeling portfolio growth scenarios. It simulates the impact of acquiring additional properties under different financing conditions, market environments, and risk profiles. This allows investors to see how each new acquisition affects overall portfolio performance. Instead of growing blindly, investors scale with precision, ensuring that each new property strengthens the system rather than diluting it.

Another powerful feature is cross-portfolio correlation analysis. In traditional investing, properties are often viewed independently. However, in reality, they are interconnected. Market downturns in one region may affect multiple assets simultaneously. AI systems analyze these correlations to identify systemic risk exposure. This helps investors avoid overconcentration in a single market or strategy and build more resilient portfolios that can withstand economic fluctuations. AI also plays a major role in exit strategy optimization. Selling a property is not just about timing the market; it is about understanding when an asset no longer contributes optimally to portfolio performance. AI evaluates long-term projections, cash flow efficiency, and opportunity cost to determine whether holding or selling an asset creates more value. This allows investors to make exit decisions based on data rather than emotion or market speculation.

Another important aspect of AI portfolio scaling is automation of reporting and decision support. Instead of manually compiling reports or reviewing spreadsheets, investors receive automated performance summaries that highlight key insights, risks, and opportunities. These reports are continuously updated and can be customized based on investor goals. This reduces administrative workload and allows investors to focus on strategic decision-making rather than operational tracking.

Integration with tools like Buildium and AppFolio enhances this system further by connecting property management operations directly into AI analysis layers. Rent collection, maintenance requests, tenant communication, and financial reporting all feed into the AI system, creating a real-time feedback loop. This ensures that portfolio decisions are always based on current data rather than outdated reports. As investors begin using AI portfolio scaling systems, their role begins to shift. They are no longer property managers or deal analysts in the traditional sense. Instead, they become system operators. Their primary function is to guide strategy, define goals, and interpret high-level insights while the AI handles execution-level analysis. This shift dramatically increases leverage, allowing a single investor to manage portfolios that would traditionally require entire teams.

Over time, this leads to exponential growth potential. Because decisions are faster, data is more accurate, and operations are more efficient, investors can scale more aggressively while maintaining control. The system itself becomes a compounding engine for wealth creation, where each new property is automatically integrated into a larger intelligence framework.

Ultimately, AI portfolio scaling represents the final evolution of real estate investing in this series. It moves beyond individual deal analysis, beyond predictive modeling, and beyond risk scoring into full system-level wealth management. Investors are no longer managing properties—they are managing intelligent portfolios that continuously optimize themselves.

### *The Investor Who Built a System That Never Slept*

When Andre started investing in real estate, he thought success meant owning a few good properties and managing them well. For years, that was exactly what he did. He acquired one property at a time, analyzed each deal carefully, and focused on maintaining steady cash flow. His portfolio grew slowly but consistently, and he took pride in being hands-on with every decision.

But as his portfolio expanded, something began to change. What once felt manageable started to feel overwhelming. Each new property added more complexity. More maintenance requests, more financial tracking, more tenant issues, more spreadsheets. Andre found himself spending more time managing his portfolio than growing it. He was working harder, but not necessarily smarter.

One night, after reviewing yet another series of reports, Andre realized something uncomfortable. He was no longer building wealth efficiently. He was managing chaos.

A colleague introduced him to an AI portfolio scaling system that promised to integrate all properties into a single intelligent framework. At first, Andre was skeptical. He had always believed real estate required personal oversight and hands-on control. The idea of automating portfolio management felt risky.

But curiosity pushed him to try it.

He connected a small portion of his portfolio to the system—just five properties at first. Within hours, the system began compiling data, analyzing performance, and generating insights he had never seen before. Instead of isolated property reports, he now saw a unified dashboard showing total portfolio performance, risk exposure, cash flow trends, and equity growth projections.

It felt like looking at his entire business from a new perspective.

Over the next few weeks, Andre added more properties to the system. As data integration expanded, the AI began identifying patterns he had never noticed. One property was consistently underperforming due to rising maintenance costs. Another was outperforming projections and had strong refinancing potential. The system even highlighted that his portfolio was overly concentrated in one geographic area, increasing his exposure to local market risk.

For the first time, Andre wasn't guessing where his weaknesses were.

He could see them clearly.

Then came the moment that changed everything.

The system recommended restructuring part of his portfolio. It suggested refinancing two properties to unlock equity and reinvesting that capital into a higher-performing market it had identified based on long-term growth projections. It also recommended adjusting rent levels on select properties to optimize cash flow without increasing vacancy risk.

Andre hesitated.

This level of decision-making used to take him weeks of analysis. Now the system was presenting it in minutes.

After reviewing the data, he followed the recommendation.

The results were immediate and measurable. Cash flow improved. Equity increased. Portfolio risk decreased. But more importantly, Andre realized something deeper was happening. He was no longer making dozens of small decisions every week. Instead, he was guiding a system that was making thousands of micro-adjustments automatically.

His role had changed.

He was no longer managing properties.

He was managing intelligence.

Months later, Andre looked at his portfolio dashboard and barely recognized the way it functioned. Properties were being optimized continuously. Maintenance issues were predicted before they became problems. Financial performance was being tracked and adjusted in real time. Even expansion opportunities were being identified automatically based on capital availability and market conditions.

One evening, he sat in silence watching the system update itself. New data flowed in. Adjustments were made. Performance indicators shifted. Everything was moving without his direct intervention.

And yet, everything was improving.

That was the moment Andre understood the truth.

He had not just built a real estate portfolio.

He had built a system that never slept, never stopped learning, and never stopped optimizing.

And for the first time, his wealth was no longer limited by his time.

*Chapter 8*

# AI Real Estate Financing Systems and Intelligent Capital Structuring

Real estate investing does not begin with property—it begins with capital. No matter how strong a deal may appear, it cannot be executed without the right financing structure in place. Traditionally, investors have treated financing as a separate step in the investment process, often approaching lenders after identifying a deal and then attempting to "make the numbers work." This reactive approach creates unnecessary friction, delays, and missed opportunities. AI real estate financing systems fundamentally change this process by turning capital planning into a proactive, integrated part of deal discovery and evaluation.

At its core, AI-driven financing is about matching the right capital structure to the right investment opportunity in real time. Instead of investors searching for loans after finding a property, AI systems evaluate financing options simultaneously with deal analysis. This creates a unified decision-making process where property selection, loan structure, cash flow, and risk exposure are all considered together. The result is a far more efficient and strategic approach to real estate investing where financing is no longer a bottleneck but a built-in advantage.

One of the most important innovations in AI financing systems is loan scenario optimization. Every real estate deal can be financed in multiple ways—conventional loans, DSCR loans, non-QM loans, HELOCs, private lending, or hybrid structures. Each option carries different interest rates, qualification requirements, down payment structures, and long-term implications. Traditionally, investors would manually compare these options one by one. AI systems automate this process by modeling multiple financing scenarios simultaneously and showing how each one impacts cash flow, ROI, and long-term equity growth.

Another key component is DSCR-based financing intelligence. Debt Service Coverage Ratio loans are particularly important for investment properties because they rely on property income rather than personal income. AI systems analyze projected rental income, expense ratios, and market stability to determine whether a property qualifies for DSCR financing and at what terms. This allows investors to quickly identify properties that are not only good investments but also easily financeable under income-based lending criteria.

AI also plays a critical role in borrower profile optimization. Instead of treating financing as a fixed process, AI systems analyze investor financial profiles—including credit score, income structure, existing debt, and asset base—to determine the most favorable lending strategies. This can include recommending whether to improve credit positioning before applying, restructure debt to increase borrowing capacity, or leverage business entities for better loan terms. In this way, financing becomes a strategic process rather than a static approval event.

Interest rate sensitivity modeling is another powerful feature of AI financing systems. Interest rates have a direct impact on cash flow and long-term returns, yet many investors underestimate this relationship. AI systems simulate how changes in interest rates affect each deal under consideration. This allows investors to understand whether a property remains profitable under higher-rate environments or whether it is overly dependent on favorable lending conditions. This type of analysis is critical for long-term stability, especially in volatile economic cycles.

AI also enables intelligent leverage structuring. Leverage is one of the most powerful tools in real estate investing, but it must be used carefully. Too much leverage increases risk, while too little can limit growth potential. AI systems analyze portfolio composition and recommend optimal leverage levels for each deal and across the entire portfolio. This includes balancing short-term cash flow needs with long-term equity accumulation strategies.

Another major advantage of AI financing systems is capital stacking optimization. Many advanced real estate investors combine multiple funding sources to structure deals more efficiently. This may include a combination of primary loans, secondary financing, HELOCs, private capital, or seller financing. AI systems evaluate how these components can be layered together to minimize cost of capital while maximizing flexibility and return. This creates financing structures that would be difficult or time-consuming to design manually.

Prequalification automation is also a key innovation. Instead of manually applying for loans and waiting for approvals, AI systems can pre-evaluate deals against lender criteria before submission. This includes analyzing property type, loan-to-value ratios, income projections, and borrower qualifications. As a result, investors can focus only on financing options that are highly likely to be approved, reducing time waste and increasing deal execution speed.

AI financing systems also improve decision alignment between acquisition and funding strategy. In traditional investing, investors often separate property selection from financing decisions, which can lead to mismatches between deal structure and loan structure. AI eliminates this disconnect by evaluating both simultaneously. This ensures that every property is acquired with a financing strategy already optimized for that specific deal.

Another important feature is refinance timing prediction. Refinancing is a critical wealth-building tool, but timing it incorrectly can reduce returns or limit capital efficiency. AI systems analyze interest rate trends, equity accumulation, and market conditions to identify optimal refinance windows. This allows investors to extract equity or improve loan terms at the most financially advantageous moments.

AI also enhances risk management in financing by identifying overexposure to certain loan types or lenders. For example, a portfolio heavily dependent on variable-rate financing may be vulnerable to interest rate increases. AI systems flag these exposures and recommend diversification strategies to stabilize debt structures. This ensures that financing risk is distributed rather than concentrated.

Integration with tools like mortgage calculators, ChatGPT, and lender databases allows AI systems to function as full financing intelligence platforms. Mortgage calculators provide baseline financial modeling, lender databases supply real-time loan product availability, and AI systems interpret and optimize all inputs into actionable financing strategies. ChatGPT further enhances this by translating complex financial structures into clear explanations that investors can understand and act upon.

As investors begin using AI financing systems, their approach to real estate fundamentally changes. Instead of asking whether they can afford a property, they begin asking how they should structure it for maximum efficiency. Financing is no longer a barrier—it becomes a strategic tool for scaling wealth. Investors begin to think in terms of capital efficiency, not just deal acquisition.

Over time, AI financing intelligence leads to more sophisticated investment strategies. Investors begin structuring deals with long-term scalability in mind, using financing not just to acquire properties but to accelerate portfolio growth. They begin leveraging equity across multiple properties, recycling capital strategically, and optimizing debt structures dynamically.

Ultimately, AI real estate financing systems represent the convergence of capital strategy and investment intelligence. They remove friction from the lending process, eliminate uncertainty from financing decisions, and transform capital into a scalable, optimized resource. In this system, financing is no longer something that slows investors down—it is what allows them to scale faster than ever before.

*The Investor Who Learned to Control Capital*

When Marcus first started investing in real estate, he believed the hardest part was finding good deals. He spent years studying neighborhoods, analyzing properties, and negotiating purchases. But no matter how good a deal looked on paper, everything always came down to one final hurdle: financing. Sometimes the bank approved his loan quickly. Other times, he lost deals because financing took too long or terms didn't work in his favor.

Marcus began to realize that financing, not deal sourcing, was actually the bottleneck in his investing process.

One afternoon, after losing yet another property due to delayed loan approval, Marcus met an investor who approached financing in a completely different way. Instead of treating loans as something to apply for after finding a property, the investor used an AI financing system that modeled loan structures in real time alongside deal analysis.

Marcus was intrigued but skeptical.

That evening, he decided to test the system on a property he was currently evaluating. It was a small multifamily building that looked promising. Instead of immediately contacting lenders like he normally would, he entered the property details into the AI platform.

Within seconds, the system generated multiple financing scenarios.

One scenario showed a conventional loan with moderate interest rates and stable cash flow. Another showed a DSCR loan that allowed qualification based on rental income instead of personal income. A third scenario combined a HELOC with a primary loan structure, optimizing cash flow while reducing upfront capital requirements.

Marcus had never seen anything like it.

He stared at the screen, realizing he wasn't just looking at financing options—he was looking at strategies.

Over the next few days, Marcus began testing more deals through the system. Each time, he noticed something important. Financing was no longer a final step in the process. It was part of the evaluation itself. Some deals that looked attractive became less appealing once financing was modeled. Others that seemed average became far more attractive when structured correctly.

For the first time, Marcus understood that the deal and the financing were not separate decisions—they were one unified system. The turning point came when he applied the system to a deal he had almost given up on. A property he liked had previously fallen through because traditional financing terms didn't work. But when he ran it through the AI system, a new structure appeared. By combining a DSCR loan with a secondary financing layer, the system showed that the deal could not only be approved but could also generate positive cash flow from day one.

Marcus immediately contacted his lender with the recommended structure.

This time, the deal closed.

Months later, Marcus reviewed his portfolio with the same system. He noticed that his most successful investments were not just good properties—they were properties that had been financed correctly. The difference between average returns and strong returns often came down to structure, not just price.

One evening, Marcus sat in his office looking at his updated financing dashboard. Every property in his portfolio was mapped with loan types, interest rates, equity positions, and refinance opportunities. The system was actively suggesting ways to improve capital efficiency across his entire portfolio.

For the first time, Marcus wasn't reacting to lenders.

He was designing financing strategies before deals were even made.

And in that moment, he realized something powerful.

He had stopped chasing approvals.

And started controlling capital itself.

*Chapter 9*

# AI Portfolio Intelligence and Automated Real Estate Scaling Systems

At a certain level of real estate investing, individual deal analysis, financing optimization, and risk scoring are no longer enough to create exponential growth. The true transition from investor to wealth builder happens when properties are no longer managed as isolated assets, but as part of a fully integrated portfolio intelligence system. This is where AI portfolio intelligence becomes the central operating engine of modern real estate wealth creation. Instead of focusing on single transactions, investors begin to manage systems of assets that continuously analyze themselves, adjust performance, and optimize capital allocation in real time.

Traditional portfolio management relies heavily on periodic reviews. Investors or property managers look at monthly or quarterly reports, identify underperforming assets, and make manual adjustments. This approach is inherently slow and reactive. By the time a problem is identified, financial inefficiencies have often already accumulated. AI portfolio intelligence eliminates this delay by continuously monitoring every property in real time and providing immediate insights into performance changes, risk exposure, and optimization opportunities.

At the core of AI portfolio intelligence is centralized asset visibility. Instead of viewing each property separately, AI systems combine all assets into a single unified dashboard that tracks cash flow, equity growth, debt exposure, occupancy rates, maintenance costs, and market performance simultaneously. This creates a living financial ecosystem where every property is connected and evaluated not just individually, but as part of a larger strategic structure. Investors are no longer managing properties—they are managing interconnected financial systems.

One of the most powerful features of AI portfolio intelligence is automated performance optimization. Each property is continuously evaluated against performance benchmarks based on its location, property type, financing structure, and market conditions. When a property underperforms relative to expectations, the system identifies the cause—whether it is low rental pricing, high expenses, inefficient financing, or market changes—and recommends corrective actions. These recommendations can include rent adjustments, refinancing opportunities, cost reductions, or even strategic disposition of the asset. Another critical component is dynamic cash flow balancing across the portfolio. In traditional investing, cash flow is often viewed at the individual property level. However,

AI systems analyze cash flow at the portfolio level, identifying how income and expenses interact across all assets. This allows investors to smooth out volatility by balancing strong-performing properties with weaker ones. In advanced systems, AI can even suggest capital reallocation strategies to improve overall portfolio stability and liquidity.

AI portfolio intelligence also introduces predictive maintenance forecasting. Instead of reacting to maintenance issues after they occur, AI systems analyze property age, system lifecycle data, historical repair patterns, and environmental factors to predict future maintenance needs. This allows investors to proactively allocate reserves, schedule repairs, and avoid unexpected capital disruptions. Over time, this significantly reduces operational inefficiency and protects long-term returns.

Another major advantage is automated equity tracking and leverage optimization. Equity is one of the most powerful wealth-building components in real estate, but it is often underutilized. AI systems continuously track equity growth across all properties and identify opportunities to extract, reinvest, or leverage that equity strategically. This includes identifying optimal refinance timing, suggesting cash-out strategies, and highlighting properties that can be used as capital sources for new acquisitions. AI portfolio intelligence also enables strategic diversification analysis. Many investors unintentionally concentrate risk in specific markets, property types, or financing structures. AI systems analyze portfolio composition and identify overexposure patterns. For example, if too many properties are located in a single region or rely on similar tenant demographics, the system flags this as concentration risk. It then recommends diversification strategies to improve long-term stability and resilience.

Another key function is automated acquisition targeting. Instead of manually searching for new deals, AI systems analyze existing portfolio performance and identify gaps in strategy. For example, if a portfolio is heavily weighted toward cash flow but lacks appreciation-driven assets, the system will recommend targeting specific types of properties or markets. This ensures that each new acquisition strengthens the overall portfolio strategy rather than simply adding more assets.

AI also enhances exit strategy intelligence by identifying optimal selling points for underperforming or mature assets. Instead of holding properties indefinitely or selling based on emotional decisions, AI evaluates long-term performance projections, market cycles, and opportunity cost to determine when an asset should be sold or repositioned. This ensures capital is always allocated to its highest and best use. Another important feature is portfolio stress testing. AI systems simulate different economic scenarios such as interest rate increases, rental market downturns, inflation spikes, or regional economic shifts. These simulations show how the entire portfolio would perform under each condition, allowing investors to identify vulnerabilities before they become real-world problems. This type of forward-looking analysis is critical for building resilient wealth systems that can withstand economic uncertainty.

Integration with property management platforms like Buildium and AppFolio further enhances portfolio intelligence by feeding real-time operational data directly into AI systems. Rent collection, tenant behavior, maintenance requests, and expense tracking are all continuously analyzed to provide up-to-date performance insights. This creates a feedback loop where operational data directly informs investment strategy.

As investors adopt AI portfolio intelligence systems, their role fundamentally changes. They are no longer focused on individual property decisions. Instead, they operate at a higher strategic level, guiding capital allocation, interpreting system recommendations, and setting long-term objectives. The AI handles execution-level analysis, while the investor focuses on direction and strategy.

Over time, this leads to exponential scalability. Investors are no longer limited by time or manual workload. A single investor can manage dozens or even hundreds of properties because the system handles continuous analysis and optimization automatically. This dramatically increases leverage, allowing for rapid portfolio growth without a proportional increase in effort.

Ultimately, AI portfolio intelligence represents the transition from active investing to system-based wealth creation. It transforms real estate from a collection of individual assets into a self-optimizing financial ecosystem. Investors no longer chase performance—they design systems that produce it continuously. This is the foundation of modern, scalable, AI-driven real estate wealth.

### *The Investor Who Stopped Managing Properties and Started Managing Systems*

When Thomas began investing in real estate, he believed success meant owning as many properties as possible and managing each one carefully. For years, he worked tirelessly analyzing deals, coordinating repairs, reviewing rental performance, and tracking expenses across his growing portfolio. At first, he enjoyed the control. He felt connected to every decision and every property. But as his portfolio expanded, the workload became overwhelming. What once felt like control slowly turned into chaos. Thomas found himself constantly reacting to problems. A tenant would move out unexpectedly, a repair bill would arrive out of nowhere, or a property would underperform without clear warning signs. Despite working harder than ever, he felt like he was losing visibility over his own portfolio. The bigger his portfolio became, the less control he actually had.

One day, while reviewing yet another set of inconsistent reports, Thomas admitted something to himself that he had been avoiding for a long time. He was no longer managing a portfolio. He was managing a collection of disconnected problems.

A fellow investor introduced him to an AI portfolio intelligence system designed to unify and automate real estate management. At first, Thomas resisted. He believed real estate required hands-on control and that automation would remove his ability to make smart decisions. But curiosity eventually pushed him to try it on a portion of his portfolio.

He connected ten properties to the system.

Within hours, everything changed.

Instead of separate reports, Thomas saw a unified dashboard showing his entire portfolio as a single system. Cash flow, equity growth, debt exposure, and occupancy rates were all displayed in real time. But what surprised him most was not the data—it was the analysis. The system began identifying patterns immediately.

One property was consistently underperforming due to rising maintenance costs. Another was generating strong cash flow but had limited long-term appreciation potential. Several properties were concentrated in the same market, increasing his exposure to regional risk. These insights had been invisible to him when viewing properties individually.

For the first time, Thomas was seeing his portfolio as a system rather than separate assets.

Over the next few weeks, he expanded the system to include his entire portfolio. As more data flowed in, the AI began making recommendations. It suggested adjusting rent levels on certain properties, refinancing others to improve cash flow, and even divesting from one asset that was dragging down overall portfolio efficiency.

Thomas hesitated at first. These were decisions he normally would have spent weeks analyzing manually. But the system showed detailed projections for each recommendation, including cash flow impact, equity changes, and long-term performance outcomes.

Eventually, he followed the guidance.

The results were immediate.

Cash flow improved across the portfolio. Risk exposure decreased. Equity growth accelerated. But the most surprising change was not financial—it was psychological. Thomas no longer felt overwhelmed. He was no longer buried in constant operational decisions. Instead, he was overseeing a system that continuously optimized itself.

One evening, Thomas sat in his office watching the portfolio dashboard update in real time. Maintenance predictions were being logged automatically. Rent adjustments were being optimized based on market conditions. Equity shifts were being tracked across all assets. The system was functioning without his constant intervention.

And yet, performance was improving.

That was the moment everything clicked.

He had spent years believing that success came from managing properties.

But now he understood something different.

Success came from managing systems that managed properties.

Months later, Thomas looked at his portfolio and barely recognized how it operated. What had once been a chaotic collection of individual assets had become a structured, intelligent system. He no longer chased problems. He no longer reacted to surprises. He no longer felt overwhelmed by scale.

Sitting back in silence, he realized the truth.

He had not just become a better investor.

He had evolved into something else entirely.

He had become the operator of a system that never stopped thinking, never stopped adjusting, and never stopped growing.

*Chapter 10*

# Building a Fully Automated AI Real Estate Wealth System

At the highest level of real estate investing, success is no longer defined by the number of properties owned, the strength of individual deals, or even the efficiency of a portfolio. True scale begins when real estate becomes a fully automated wealth system—one that continuously generates opportunities, analyzes them, finances them, and optimizes them without requiring constant manual intervention. This is the final evolution of AI real estate investing: a complete ecosystem where data, decision-making, and execution are integrated into a self-operating structure designed to build wealth continuously over time.

A fully automated AI real estate system is built on four interconnected pillars: deal generation, deal analysis, financing automation, and portfolio optimization. Each pillar functions independently, but also feeds data into the others, creating a closed-loop intelligence system. Instead of investors manually moving through each stage, AI systems handle the majority of the operational workload while the investor focuses on strategy, capital allocation, and long-term vision. This shift transforms real estate from an active business into a scalable, semi-autonomous wealth engine.

The first pillar, automated deal generation, is responsible for continuously sourcing opportunities from multiple channels. This includes MLS feeds, off-market databases, public records, direct-to-seller marketing systems, and AI-enhanced scraping tools. Instead of searching manually, investors receive a constant stream of filtered, pre-qualified opportunities that match their investment criteria. These deals are not random—they are dynamically selected based on investor preferences, portfolio gaps, and market conditions. Over time, the system becomes more refined, learning which types of deals the investor consistently accepts and which ones are ignored.

The second pillar, AI deal analysis, acts as the intelligence layer of the system. Every incoming deal is automatically evaluated for cash flow potential, risk exposure, rental projections, ARV estimates, financing feasibility, and long-term ROI. This eliminates the need for manual underwriting or spreadsheet modeling. Instead, each property is instantly converted into a structured investment profile that includes financial performance forecasts and risk-adjusted scoring. The investor is no longer overwhelmed with raw data—they are presented with fully interpreted investment opportunities. The third pillar, financing automation, connects deals directly to capital structures. Instead of evaluating financing after identifying a property, AI systems analyze financing options simultaneously during deal evaluation. This includes DSCR loans, conventional mortgages, HELOC strategies, private lending options, and hybrid capital structures. The system identifies optimal financing strategies based on investor credit profile, property type, and projected cash flow. In advanced setups, prequalification and lender matching can be automated, significantly reducing friction and closing time.

The fourth pillar, portfolio optimization, ensures that all assets operate as a unified system. Once properties are acquired, AI continuously monitors performance metrics such as cash flow, equity growth, occupancy rates, maintenance costs, and market trends. It identifies inefficiencies, suggests refinances, recommends rent adjustments, and flags underperforming assets for strategic action. Instead of static portfolio management, investors operate within a dynamic system that continuously improves itself over time.

One of the most powerful features of a fully automated AI system is capital recycling. As properties generate equity and cash flow, AI identifies opportunities to redeploy capital into new acquisitions. This creates a compounding effect where the portfolio grows not only through appreciation and rent increases but through continuous reinvestment. The system ensures that capital is never idle and is always allocated toward the highest-performing opportunities available.

Another critical component is predictive scaling intelligence. Instead of growing randomly, AI systems analyze portfolio structure and recommend specific expansion strategies. For example, if a portfolio is heavily weighted toward single-family rentals, the system may suggest diversification into multifamily or short-term rentals. If cash flow is strong but appreciation is weak, it may recommend targeting growth markets. This ensures that every expansion decision strengthens the overall portfolio rather than simply increasing size.

Automation also extends into risk management. AI continuously evaluates exposure across markets, property types, and financing structures. It identifies concentration risk, interest rate sensitivity, and liquidity constraints before they become problems. If a portfolio becomes overexposed to a specific risk factor, the system recommends corrective actions such as refinancing, selling, or diversifying assets. This proactive approach significantly reduces downside exposure and improves long-term stability.

Another key feature is autonomous performance benchmarking. Each property is continuously compared against expected performance metrics based on its category and market. If a property underperforms, the system identifies why and suggests corrective action. If a property outperforms, the system analyzes the reasons for success and applies those insights to other assets in the portfolio. This creates a continuous learning loop that improves performance across the entire system over time.

AI systems also introduce automated exit strategy execution planning. Instead of waiting for market conditions to change, investors receive predictive insights on when to hold, refinance, or sell properties based on long-term modeling. This ensures that assets are never held too long past their optimal performance window and that capital is always positioned efficiently.

Integration with external tools such as ChatGPT, DealCheck, Mashvisor, Buildium, and AppFolio enhances the automation ecosystem by connecting data sources, financial models, and operational systems into a single intelligence network. ChatGPT adds interpretive intelligence, explaining system outputs in human-readable form and assisting with strategic decision-making. Property management platforms feed real-time operational data into the system, ensuring accuracy and responsiveness.

As investors adopt fully automated AI systems, their role evolves significantly. They are no longer operators managing individual tasks. Instead, they become system architects and capital strategists. Their primary function is to set goals, define investment parameters, allocate capital, and interpret high-level insights. The AI handles execution, analysis, and optimization. This separation of roles dramatically increases leverage and scalability.

Over time, this leads to exponential wealth acceleration. Because the system continuously generates deals, analyzes opportunities, structures financing, and optimizes portfolios, growth becomes compounding and self-reinforcing. Each new property strengthens the system, and the system improves the performance of each property. This feedback loop creates a powerful engine for long-term wealth creation.

Ultimately, a fully automated AI real estate system represents the final stage of evolution in modern investing. It transforms real estate from a manual, labor-intensive business into an intelligent, self-improving financial ecosystem. Investors are no longer limited by time, bandwidth, or operational capacity. Instead, they operate systems that scale, learn, and optimize continuously. This is not just the future of real estate investing—it is the foundation of next-generation wealth creation.

### *The Man Who Built a Real Estate Machine That Replaced His Work*

When Adrian first started investing in real estate, he believed success meant constant effort. He worked long hours analyzing deals, negotiating with lenders, coordinating with contractors, and managing tenants. Every part of his business required his attention. At first, he accepted it as part of the process. He believed that if he worked harder than everyone else, he would eventually achieve financial freedom.

For years, Adrian lived in a cycle of constant activity. He was always reviewing listings, always running numbers, always chasing the next opportunity. He built a respectable portfolio, but he never felt free. His business depended entirely on him, and stepping away for even a few days would create chaos. Deep down, he knew he had not built a system—he had built a job.

One evening, after missing a family event because of an urgent property issue, Adrian reached a breaking point. He sat alone reviewing spreadsheets late at night and asked himself a difficult question: if he had to step away from everything tomorrow, would his business survive?

The answer was no.

That realization changed everything.

Shortly after, Adrian was introduced to a fully automated AI real estate system designed to handle every stage of investing. At first, he was skeptical. The idea that a system could source deals, analyze them, structure financing, and manage a portfolio seemed unrealistic. But this time, instead of dismissing it, he decided to test it on a small scale.

He connected a portion of his business to the system and watched what happened.

Within hours, deals began flowing in automatically. Each opportunity was already pre-filtered and ranked based on his investment criteria. He no longer had to search for deals—the system brought them to him.

Next, he reviewed the analysis. Every property was already fully evaluated. Cash flow projections, risk scores, financing options, and long-term ROI forecasts were all presented clearly. What used to take him hours now took seconds to understand.

Then came financing.

The system didn't just analyze deals—it suggested how to fund them. It showed him optimal loan structures, recommended DSCR options, and even identified refinance strategies he had never considered. For the first time, Adrian realized he was no longer thinking in stages. The entire investment process was happening simultaneously.

Over the next few weeks, he expanded the system across more of his portfolio. As he did, something unexpected happened. His workload didn't just decrease—it disappeared. Maintenance issues were flagged before they became problems. Rent adjustments were suggested automatically. Underperforming properties were identified with clear recommendations.

The system wasn't just managing his portfolio.

It was improving it.

One night, Adrian sat watching his dashboard update in real time. New deals were being analyzed. Portfolio performance was being optimized. Capital allocation strategies were being adjusted automatically. Everything was moving without his intervention.

He had not made a single operational decision that day.

And yet, his business had grown.

That was the moment everything shifted.

Adrian realized he was no longer running a real estate business.

He was overseeing a machine that ran itself. Months later, Adrian's life looked completely different. He no longer spent nights buried in spreadsheets or emergencies. Instead, he focused on strategy, expansion, and long-term vision. The system handled execution. He handled direction.

One afternoon, he looked at his portfolio and noticed something profound. It was no longer just a collection of properties. It had become a living system—buying, analyzing, optimizing, and scaling without hesitation.

And for the first time in his career, Adrian understood the truth.

He had not built a portfolio.

He had built a machine that created wealth while he lived his life.

# Final Comments

*The Future of AI Real Estate Investing and What Comes Next*

Reaching the end of this series is not an ending point—it is a transition point. By now, you have seen how artificial intelligence reshapes every layer of real estate investing, from deal sourcing and analysis to financing, portfolio management, scaling, and full automation. What once required teams of analysts, spreadsheets, brokers, lenders, and property managers can now be condensed into an integrated system of intelligence that operates continuously. But the real lesson is not just about technology. It is about how thinking changes when information becomes instant, decisions become structured, and execution becomes systemized.

The traditional way of investing in real estate has always been constrained by human limitations. Time, attention, emotion, and incomplete information have shaped every decision. Even experienced investors have historically relied on intuition to fill in the gaps that data could not cover. AI does not eliminate human judgment, but it removes the uncertainty that forces judgment to operate blindly. Instead of guessing, investors now evaluate. Instead of reacting, they anticipate. Instead of operating in isolation, they operate within systems that process far more information than any individual could manage alone.

One of the most important shifts you should take away from this entire framework is that real estate is no longer just about properties—it is about systems. A single property is no longer viewed as an isolated investment but as a data point within a larger portfolio intelligence structure. That structure continuously evolves based on market conditions, financing opportunities, rental dynamics, and long-term wealth projections. When you begin to see investing through this lens, your entire approach changes. You stop asking "Is this a good deal?" and start asking "How does this deal improve my system?"

Another critical transformation is the shift from effort-based success to leverage-based success. In traditional real estate investing, income is often directly tied to effort. The more deals you analyze, the more properties you manage, and the more problems you solve, the more you potentially earn. AI breaks this relationship. It introduces leverage at every stage of the process. One investor can now analyze hundreds of deals, manage a large portfolio, and optimize capital structures without increasing workload proportionally. This is not just efficiency—it is exponential leverage.

However, with this new level of leverage comes a new responsibility. When decisions are made faster and at larger scale, discipline becomes more important than ever. AI will surface opportunities constantly, but not every opportunity should be pursued. The ability to filter, prioritize, and align investments with long-term strategy becomes the true skill of the modern investor. In this environment, success is not determined by access to data, but by the clarity of the system guiding that data.

It is also important to understand that AI does not remove risk—it clarifies it. Every investment still carries uncertainty, but that uncertainty is now visible, measurable, and comparable. Risk is no longer something that hides inside assumptions or blind spots. It is structured, scored, and modeled across multiple scenarios. This allows investors to make decisions with awareness rather than ignorance. The goal is not to eliminate risk entirely, but to understand it deeply enough to control it strategically.

As you move forward from this series, one of the most powerful mindset shifts is recognizing that real estate investing is no longer a linear process. It is not simply find a deal, analyze it, finance it, and manage it. It is now a continuous loop where data flows in constantly, systems evaluate performance in real time, and capital is continuously reallocated toward higher-performing opportunities. In this loop, nothing is static. Everything is adaptive. Another key takeaway is that scale is no longer limited by personal capacity. In the past, investors reached a natural ceiling based on how many properties they could manage, how many deals they could analyze, or how many decisions they could make. AI removes that ceiling by distributing intelligence across the entire system. This allows investors to move from managing properties to managing strategies, and from managing strategies to managing entire financial ecosystems.

At the same time, it is essential to recognize that AI is not a replacement for vision. Systems can analyze, optimize, and execute—but they cannot define purpose. They cannot determine what kind of life you want to build, what level of risk you are willing to accept, or what long-term goals matter most to you. That responsibility remains human. The most successful investors in this new environment will not be the ones who rely entirely on automation, but the ones who learn how to direct it with clarity and intention.

Another important realization is that wealth creation in this new model becomes compounding at multiple levels. Not only does capital grow over time, but systems themselves improve through feedback loops. Every decision feeds data back into the system, making future decisions more accurate. Every property added improves portfolio intelligence. Every financing structure refines capital efficiency. Over time, the system becomes more valuable than any single asset within it.

This is why the future of real estate investing will not be defined by individual investors competing for deals, but by systems competing for efficiency. The investors who build the most intelligent, adaptive, and scalable systems will consistently outperform those who rely on manual processes, no matter how experienced they are. Experience will still matter, but it will matter most when combined with structured intelligence.

As you reflect on everything in this series, the most important question is not what you have learned—it is how you will apply it. Knowledge alone does not create transformation. Systems do. The real shift happens when information becomes execution, and execution becomes structure. That is where wealth begins to compound in a meaningful way.

Ultimately, AI real estate investing is not about replacing traditional investing—it is about evolving it. The fundamentals of real estate remain the same: location, cash flow, leverage, risk, and timing. What changes is how quickly and accurately those fundamentals can be evaluated and applied. AI simply removes friction from decision-making and expands the scale at which those decisions can be executed.

The future belongs to investors who think in systems, not transactions. Who think in decades, not deals. Who think in optimization, not effort. And who understand that in a world of intelligent automation, the greatest advantage is no longer information—it is structure.

This series is designed to give you that structure.

What you build with it is entirely up to you.

www.ingramcontent.com/pod-product-compliance
Ingram Content Group UK Ltd.
Pitfield, Milton Keynes, MK11 3LW, UK
UKHW010012031026
15589UKWH00008B/1621

9 798295 885143